Good Night Cryptids Everywhere!

Written by Ulrika Pillai

First Published in 2023
Text copyright © Ulrika Pillai
All rights reserved with the author.
Contact - ulrikapillai@yahoo.com

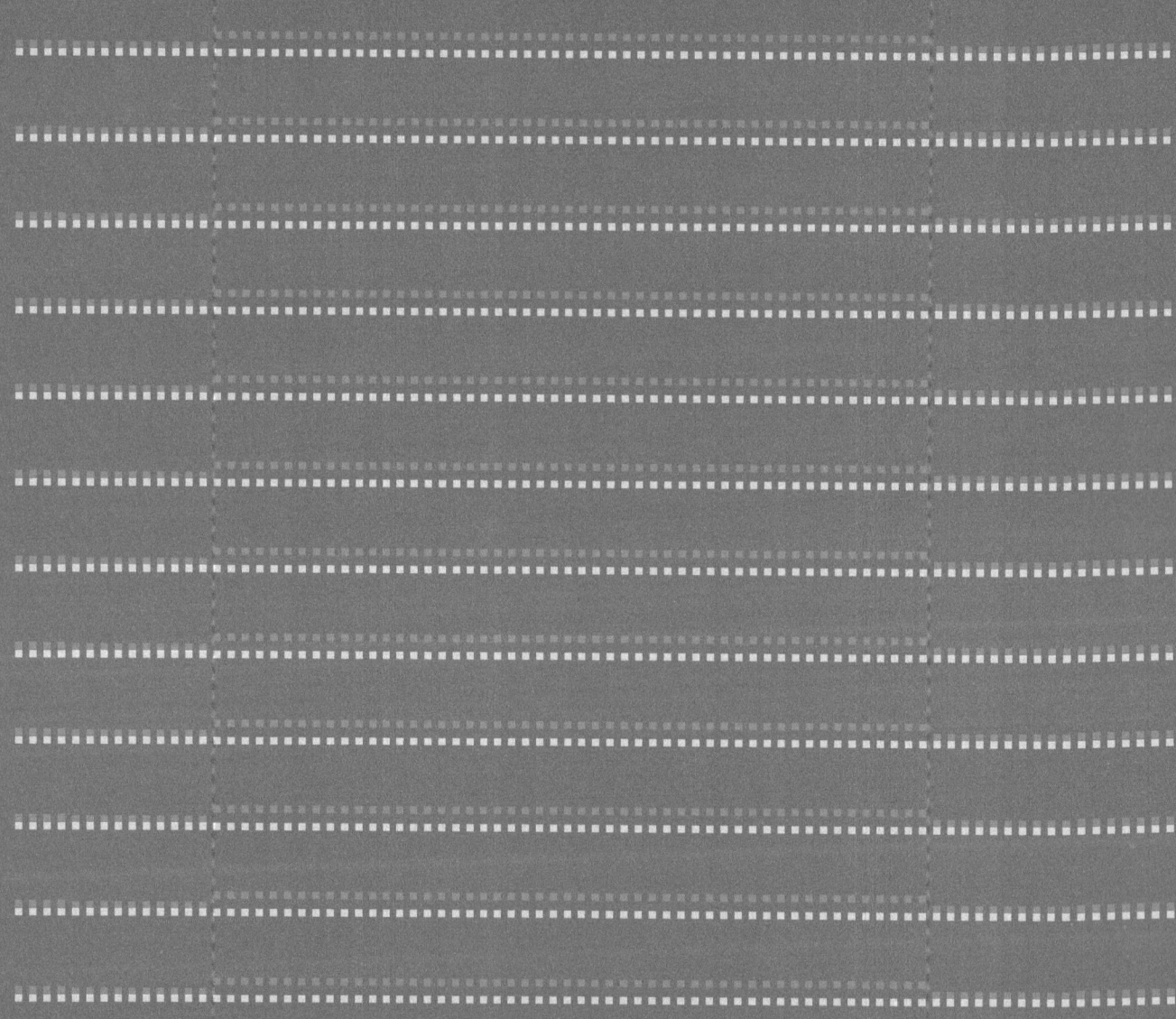

This book belongs to little monster

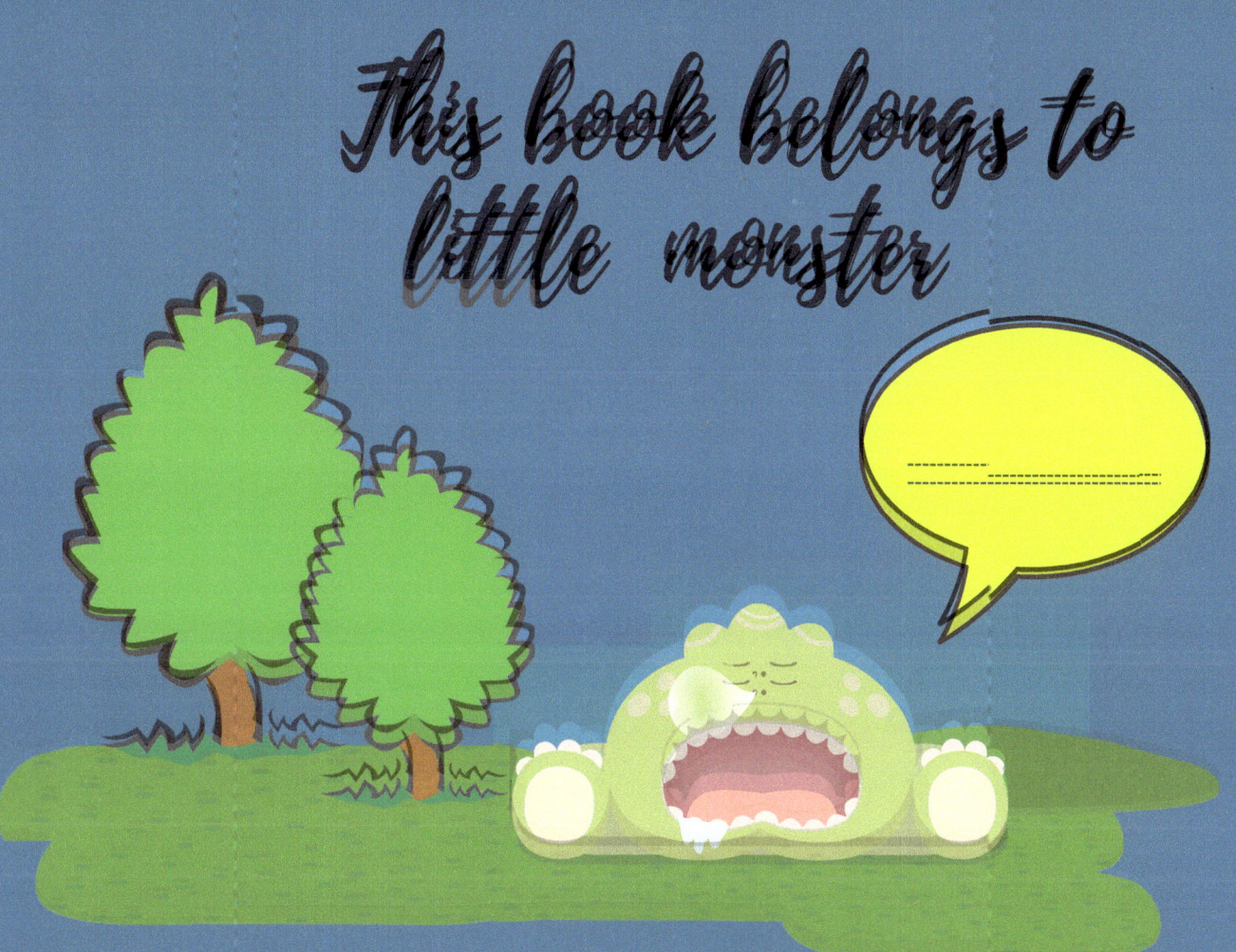

First Published in 2023
Text copyright © Ulrika Pillai
All rights reserved with the author.
Contact - ulrikapillai@yahoo.com

Special Thanks to canva.com and pixabay.com for the images provided in the free to use under the content license.

Good Night Cryptids Everywhere!

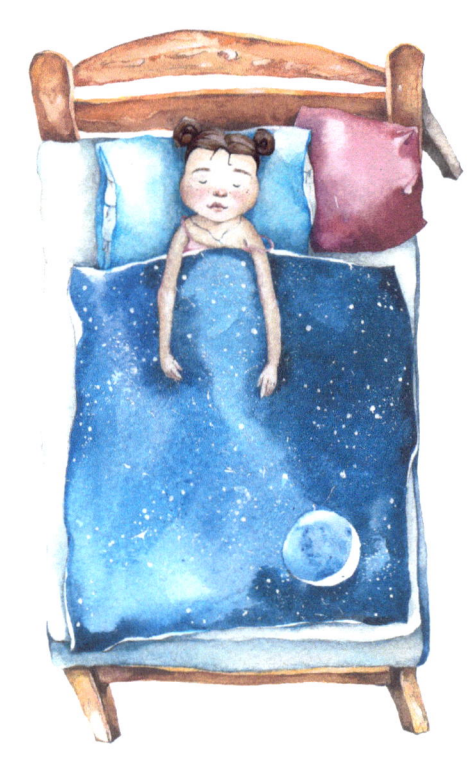

The moon is high -
Up in the sky !
Mummy tucks in Reeva
with
a soft lullaby.
But *little Reeva* jumps
back
on her feet.
"Mummy," she yells,

"I don't need any of this sleep."

Then she plays with the dolls,
the cars and the tractors too.

All loud noises go -
BEEP! BEEP! BEEP!
"OH! dear," *said Mummy.*
Loud and clear !

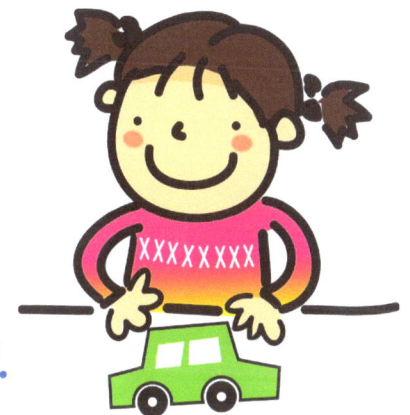

"All little monsters need their sleep!"

In Asia,
    Baby Yeti -
In his bed he hops-
    Over the snow filled - icy mountain tops.

Listening to his Mumma's voice,

And the cold wind *blowing* Swish - Swosh.

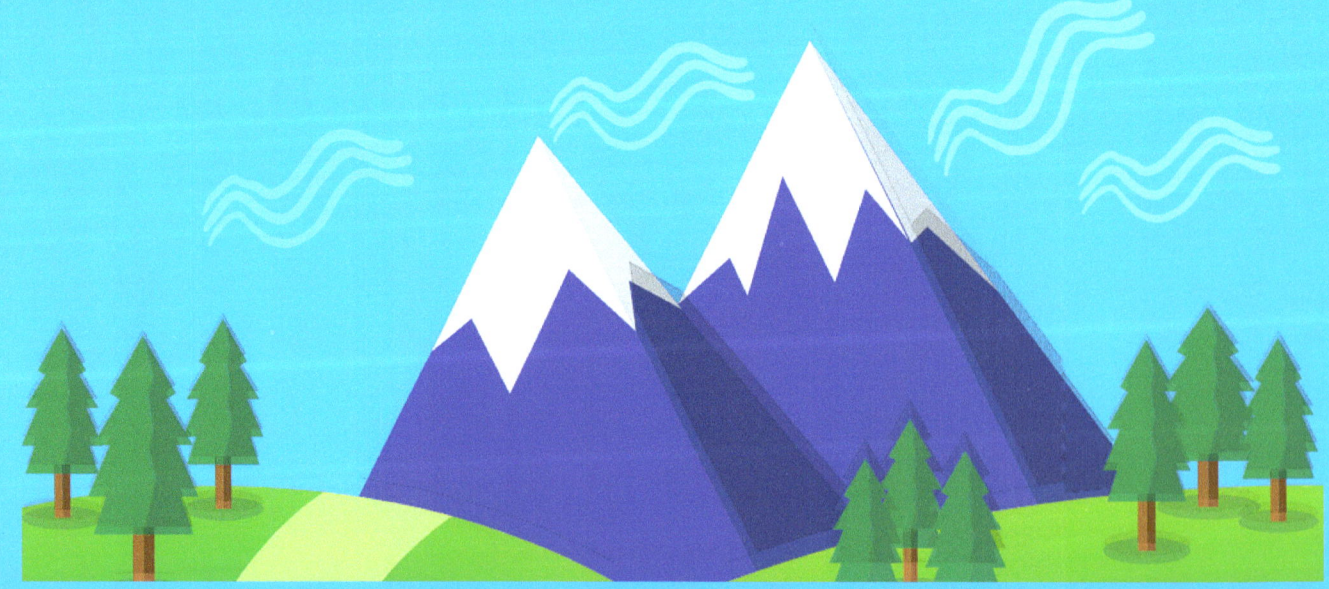

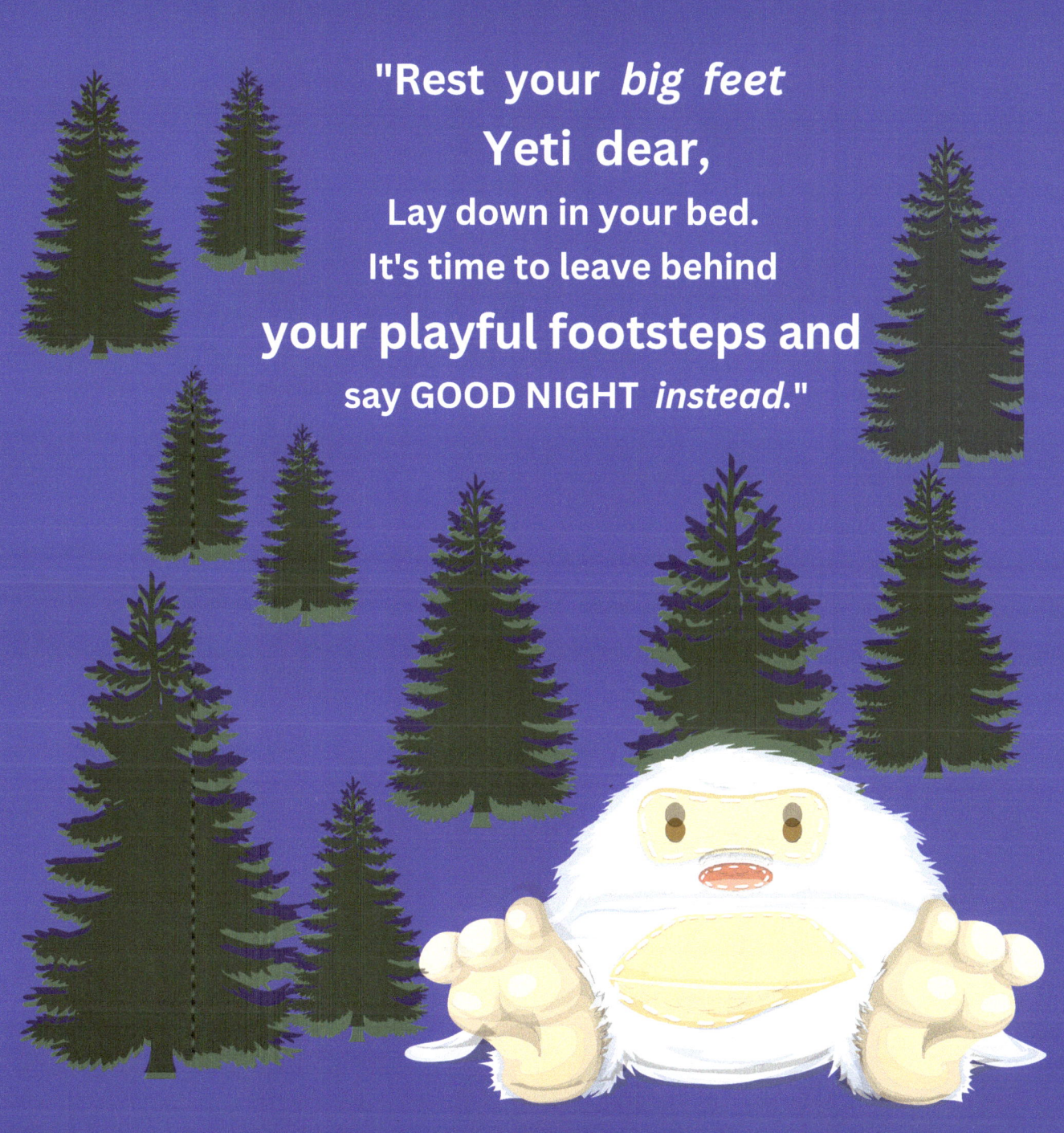

"Rest your *big feet* **Yeti dear,** Lay down in your bed. It's time to leave behind **your playful footsteps and** say GOOD NIGHT *instead.*"

In Norway,

Baby Kraken-

Wakes up to a **scary dream.**

"Can **Mr. Human** make out of me **a fish soup** with **buttery cream ?**"

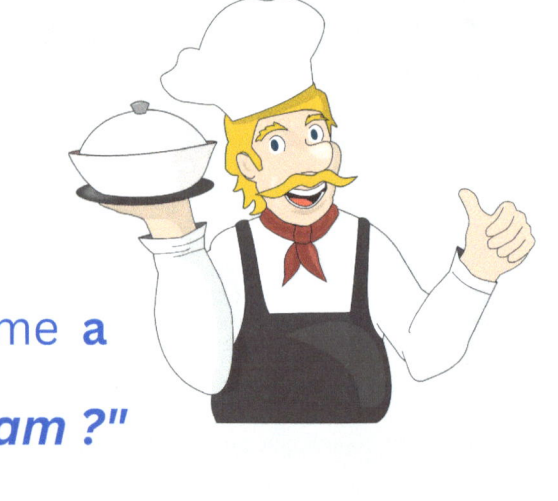

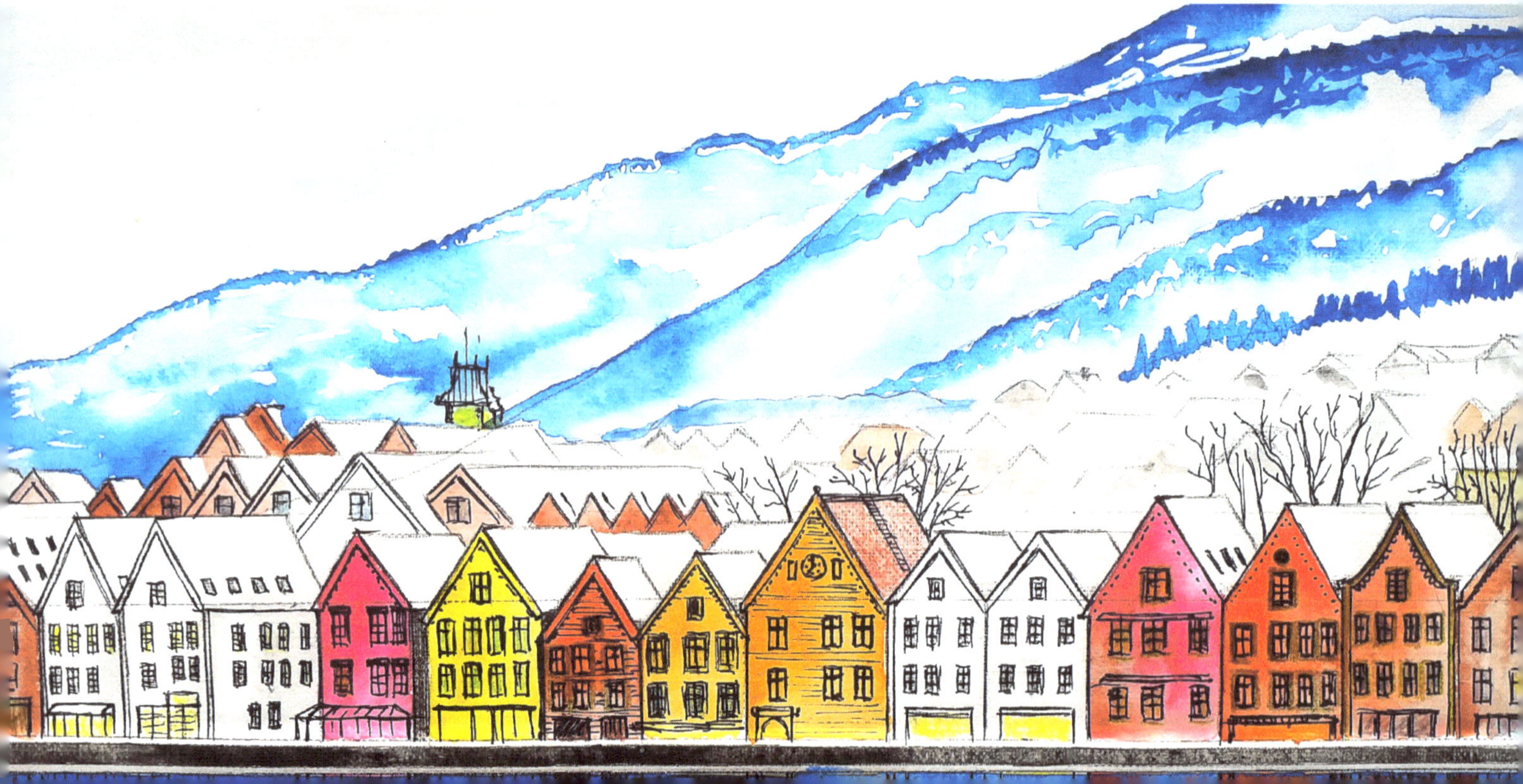

"**Oh! No!**" said Grandpa,

"Don't get hooked, these are silly tales in your story book."

Then, Baby Kraken rolls around in his watery bed-
And listens to the calming stream instead.

Sleep little baby Kraken,
Sleep,
Tomorrow is another great big feat !

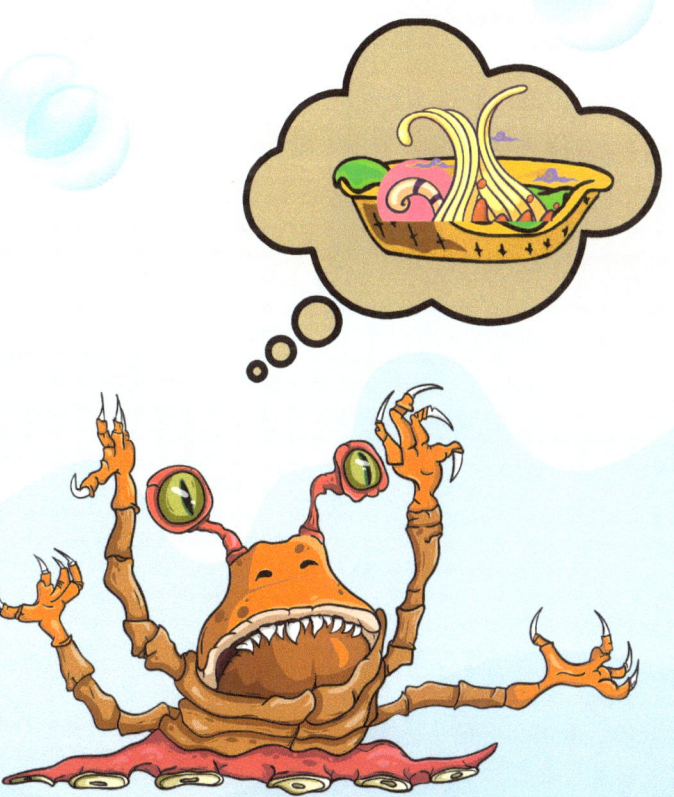

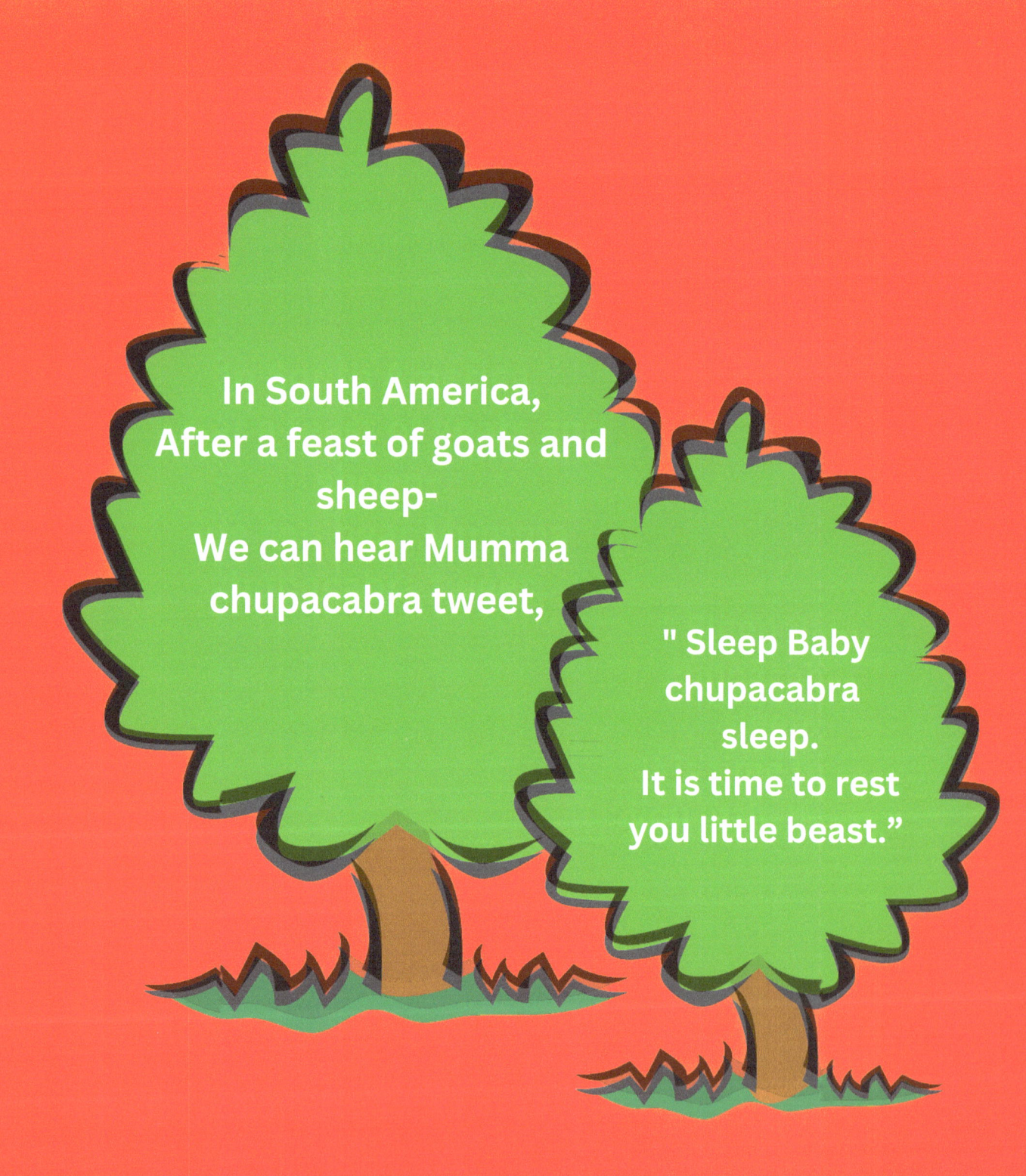

Then it lays it's head on
mumma's hairy chest.

And tries to get a
good night's rest.

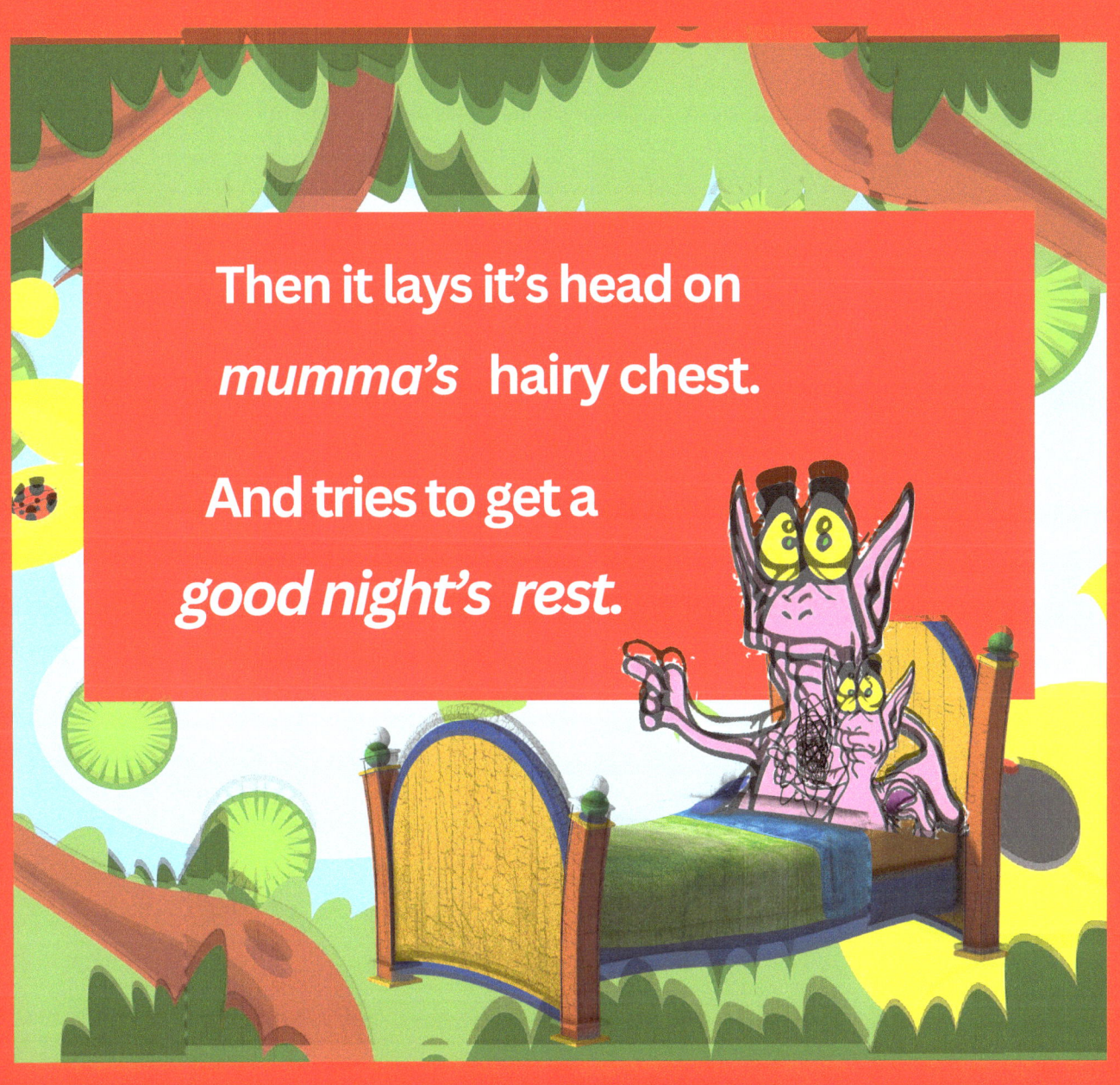

And *somewhere* in the world -
Not so far away.
Little Nessie has finished his play.
" It's time to settle down, my Nessie dear."
He can hear his *Grandma* say.

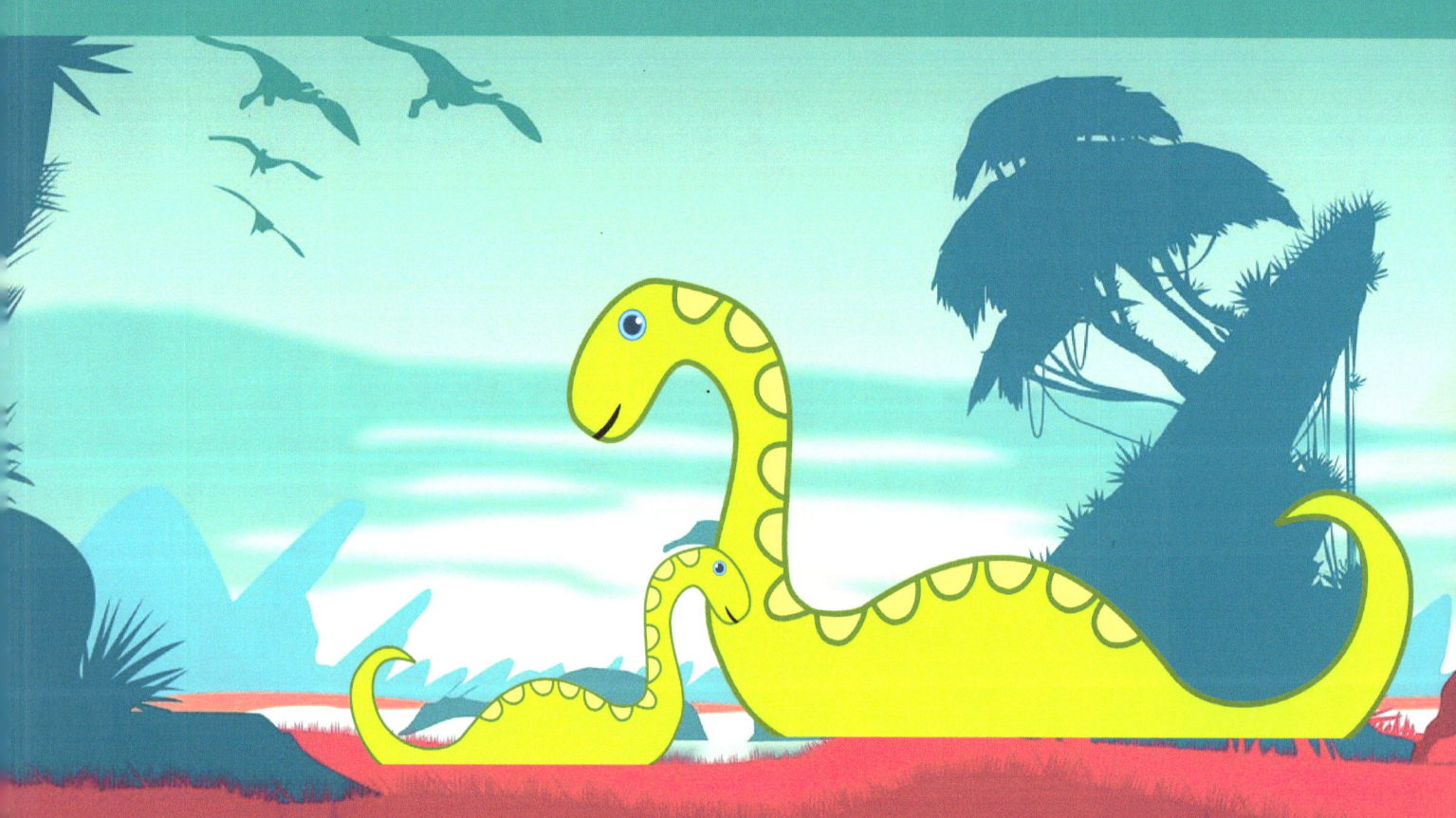

Rest your long neck
Baby Nessie,
   On the *Lockness*
watery floor.

**Wake up fresh
tomorrow,**
   It's another day for
you to explore.

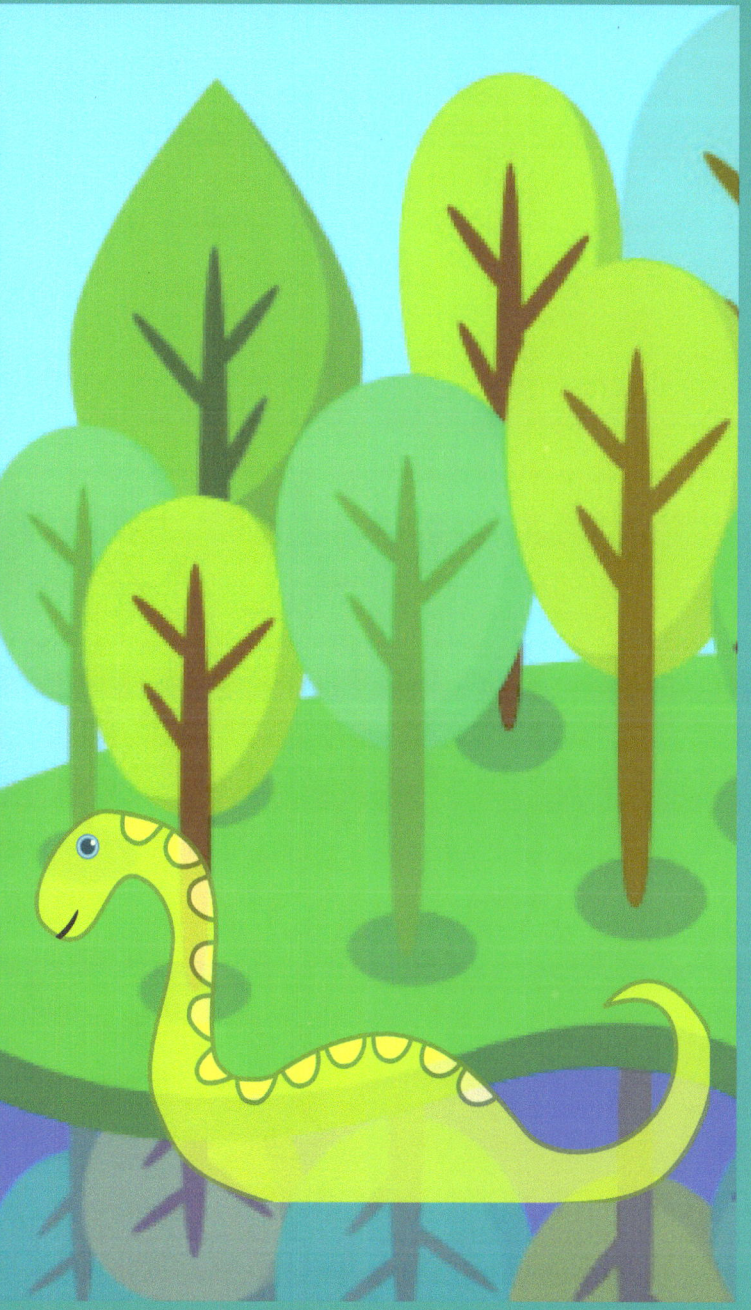

And this little red 'Yara-Ma-Yha Who'
is cradled high up on
Australia's tree top.
Can you hear its
coo?

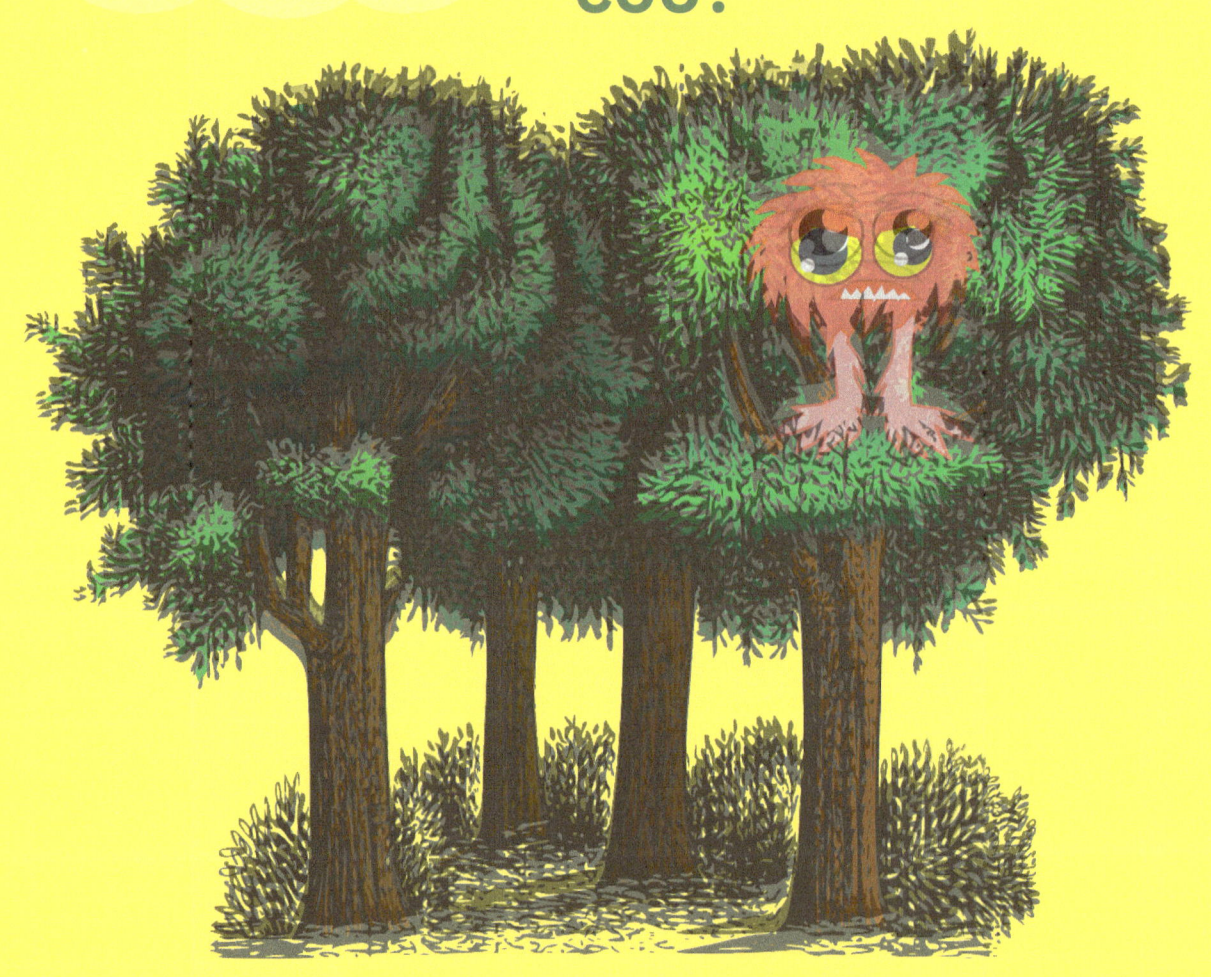

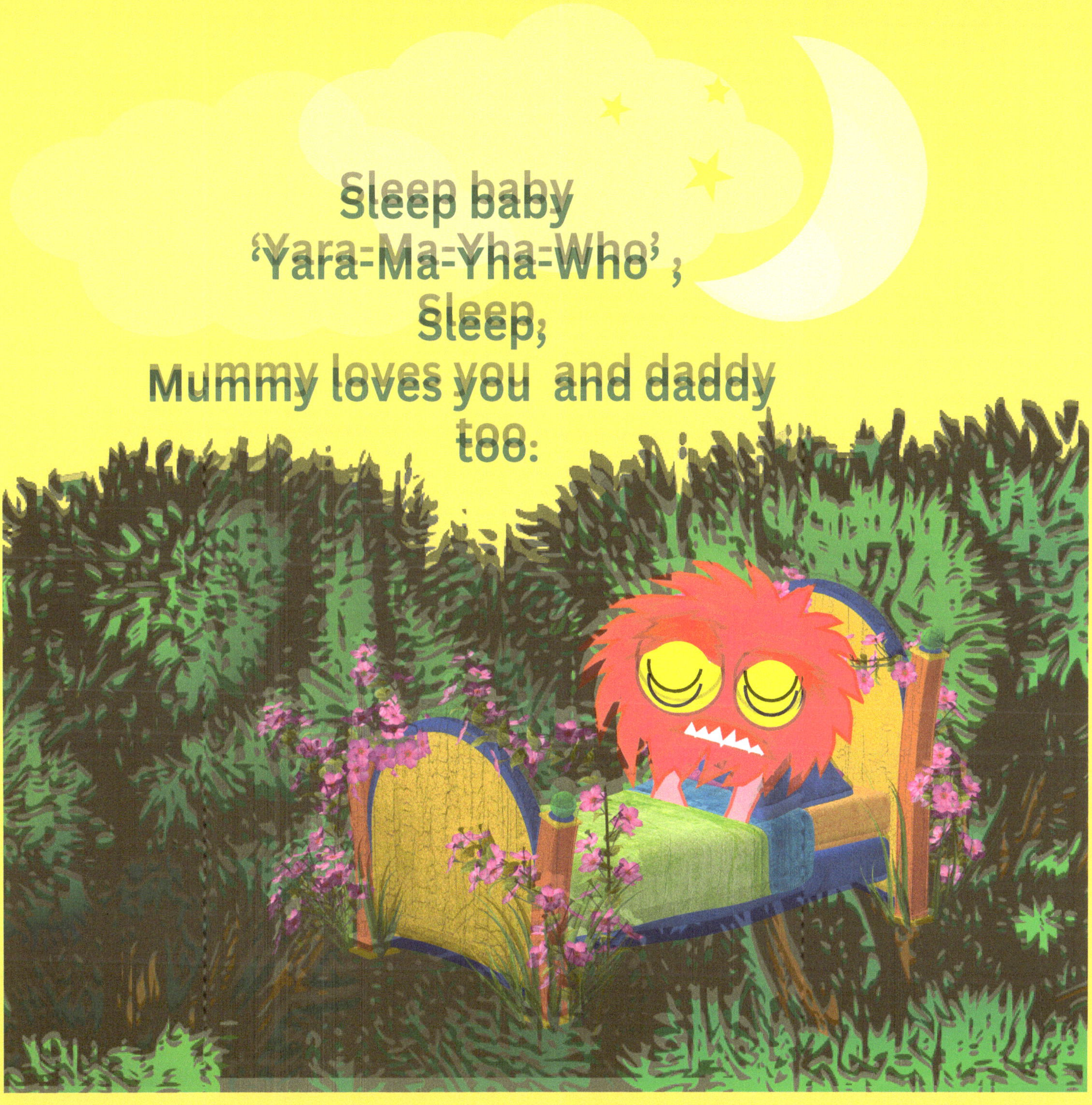

Sleep baby 'Yara-Ma-Yha-Who';
Sleep;
Mummy loves you and daddy too.

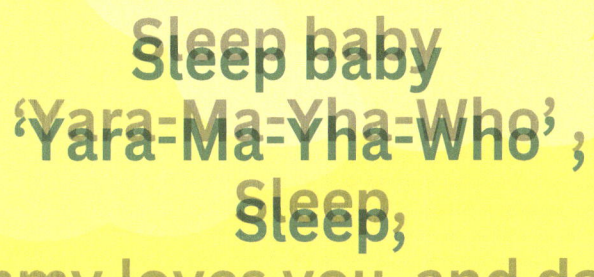

And when in North America-
It is dawn.
Behind the mountain-
The full moon's shine has gone.

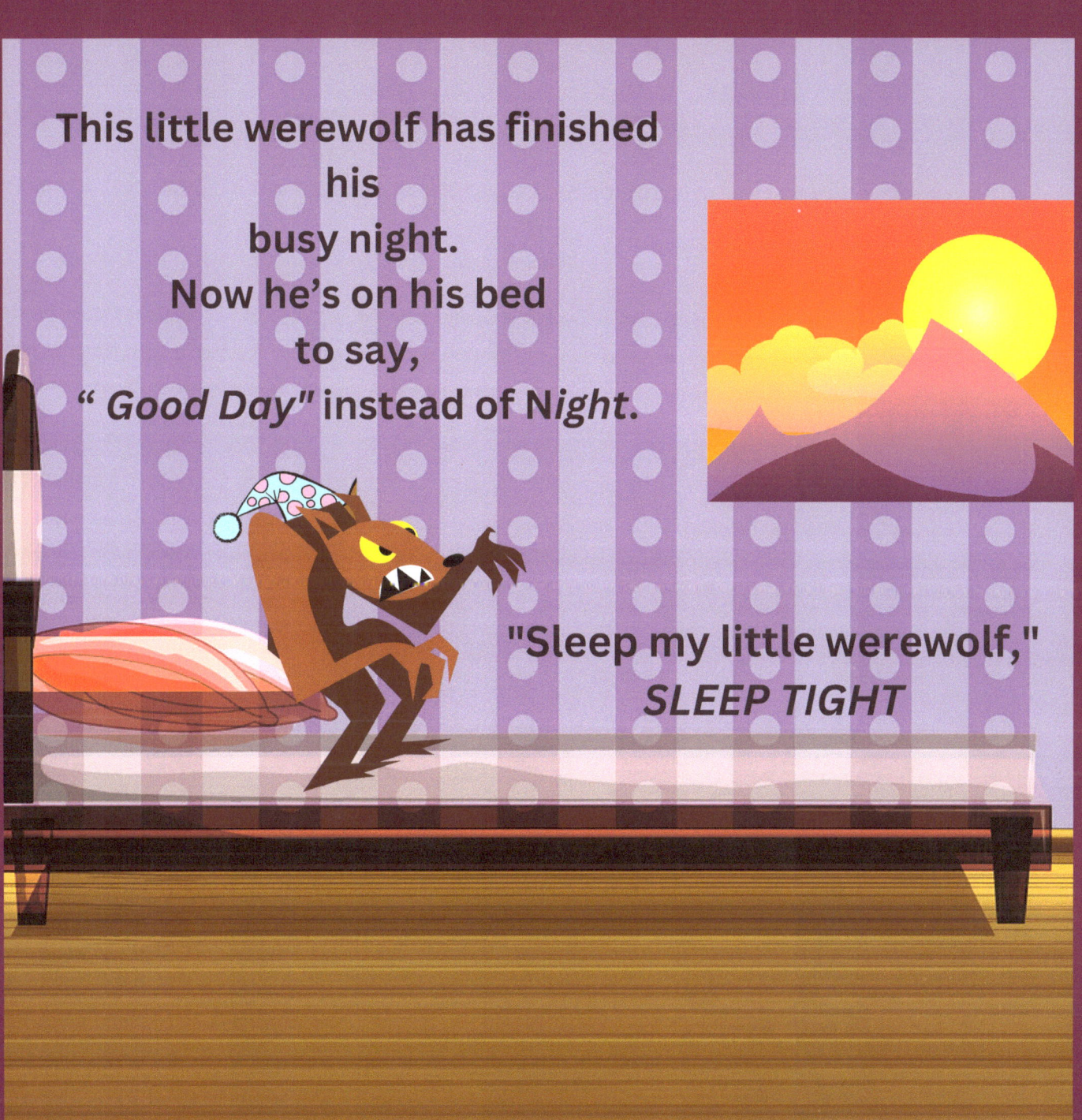

This little werewolf has finished his busy night.
Now he's on his bed to say,
" *Good Day*" instead of N*ight*.

"Sleep my little werewolf,"
SLEEP TIGHT

And in Japan's Fuji Mountain -

Way deep below .

Little Baby Dragon

shuts his wings and starts to snore.

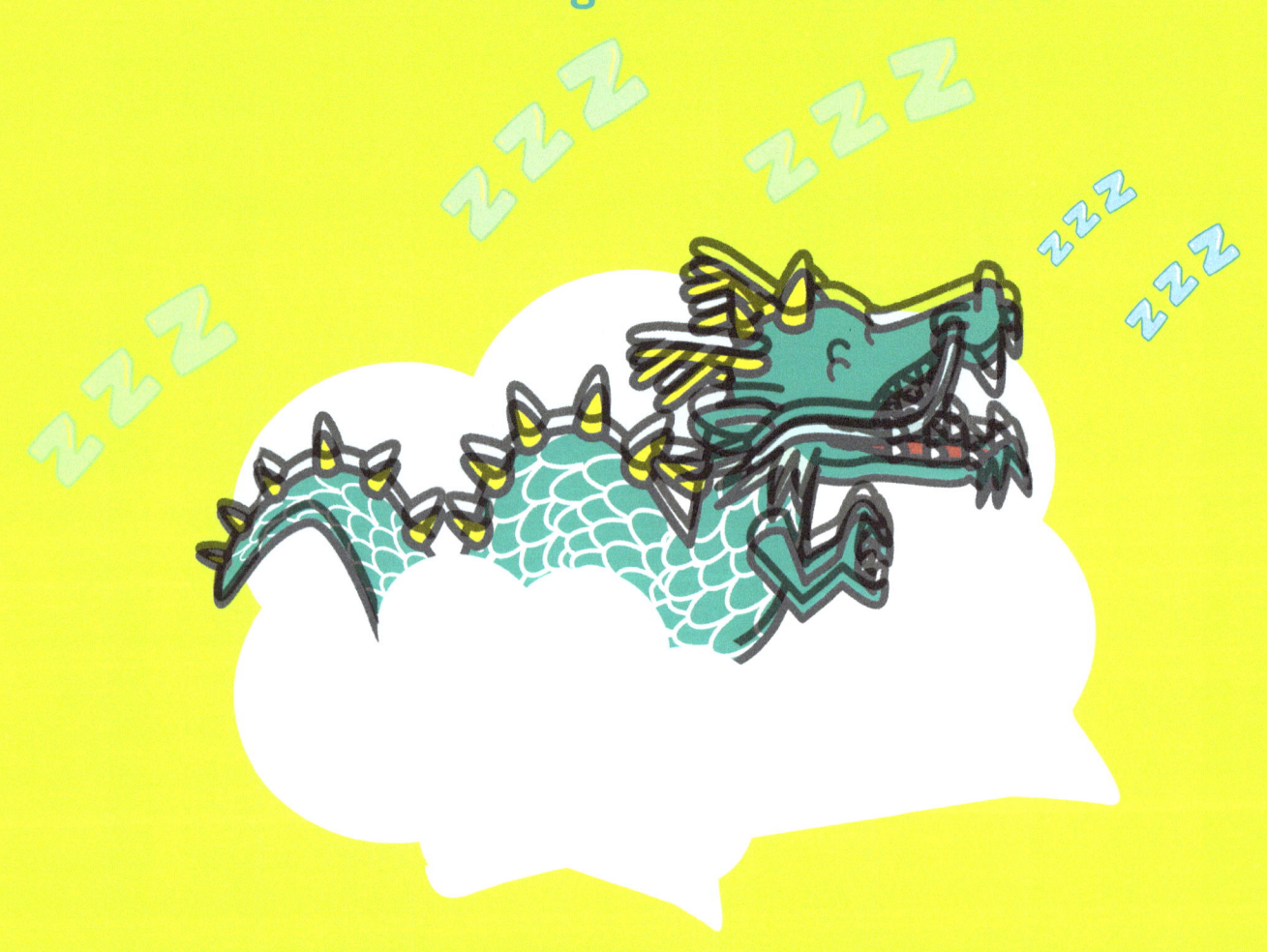

Rest your fiery breath
Baby Dragon,
Sleep well in your warm
volcano nest.
Tomorrow is another day
for you to   *soar*.

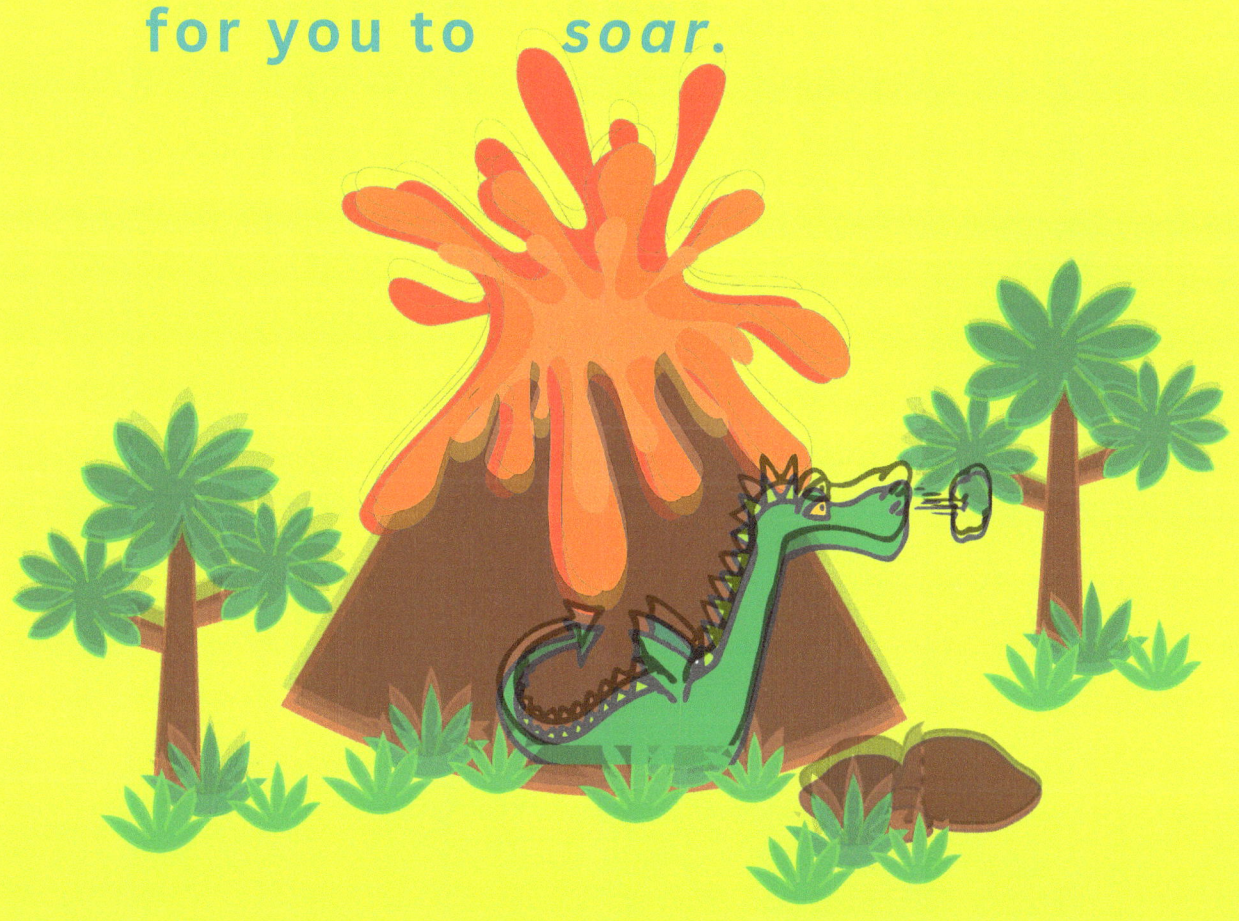

And I'm sure in all the countries-
Around the world.
Some little monster in their bed
twists and twirls.

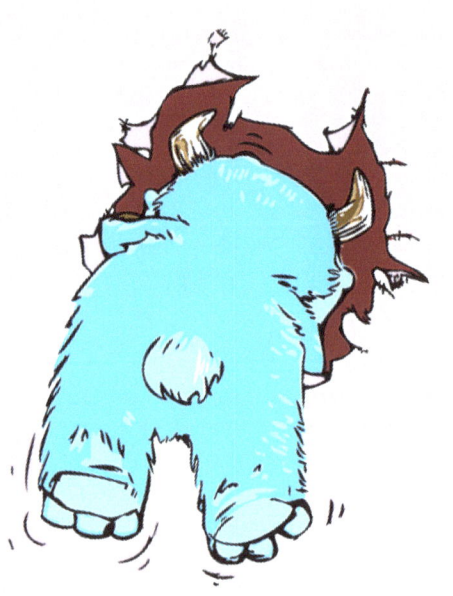

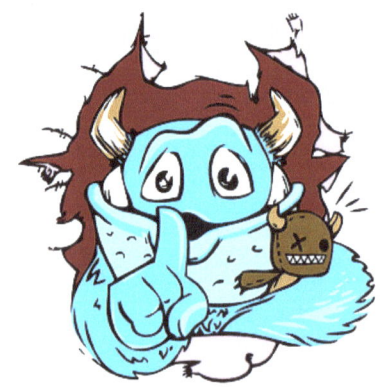

And in the night-
All tugged up tight.
Some little monster is saying,

"Good Night"

And in all the continents-
At different time zones.

All little monsters do
sleep in their homes.

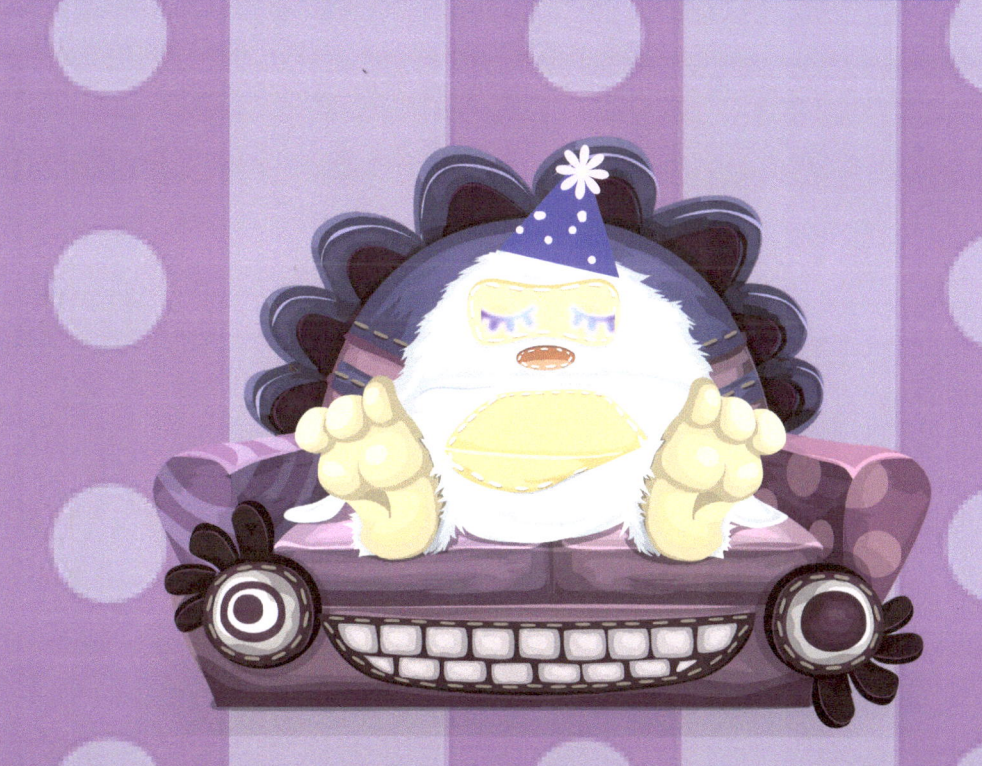

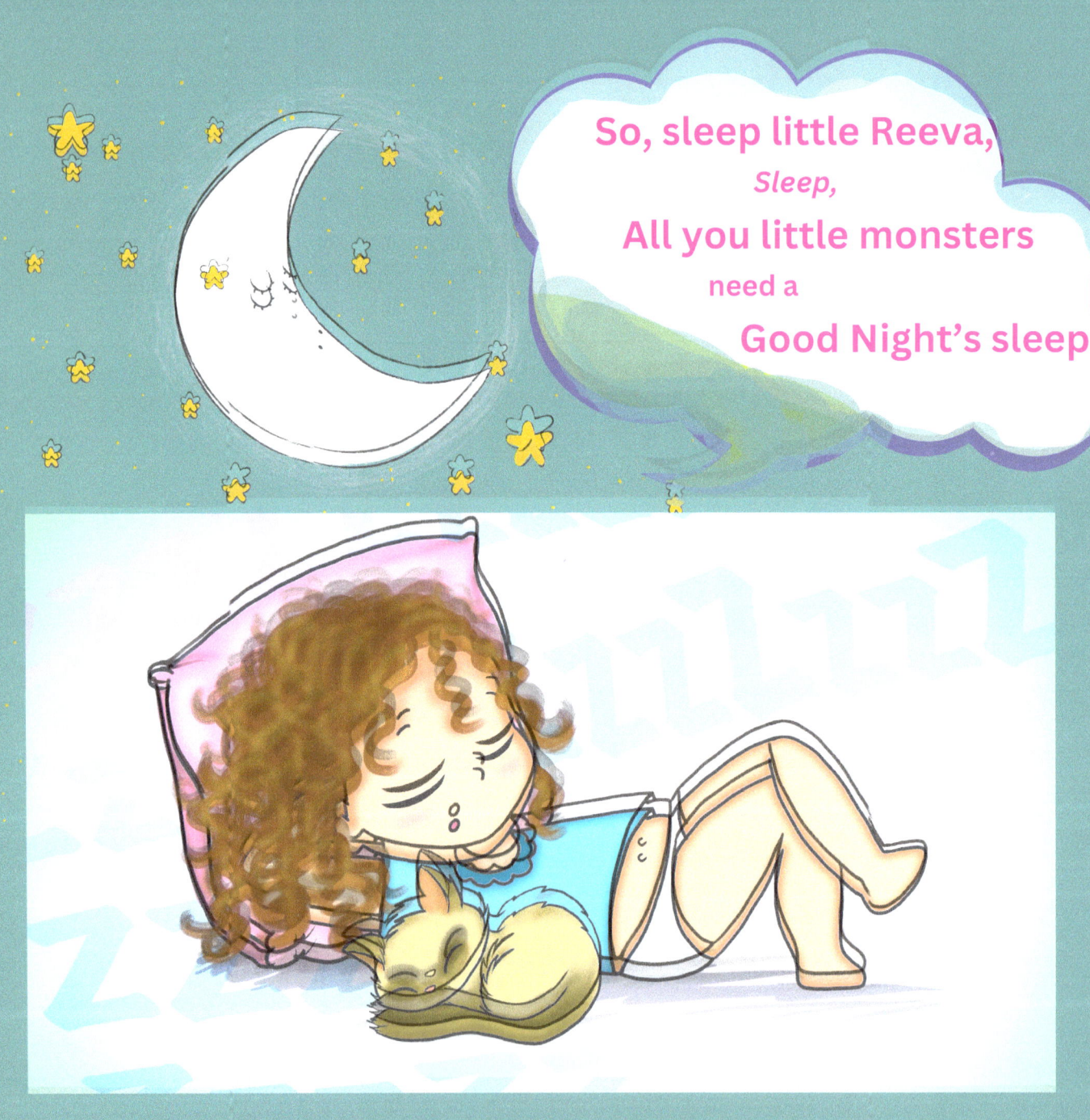

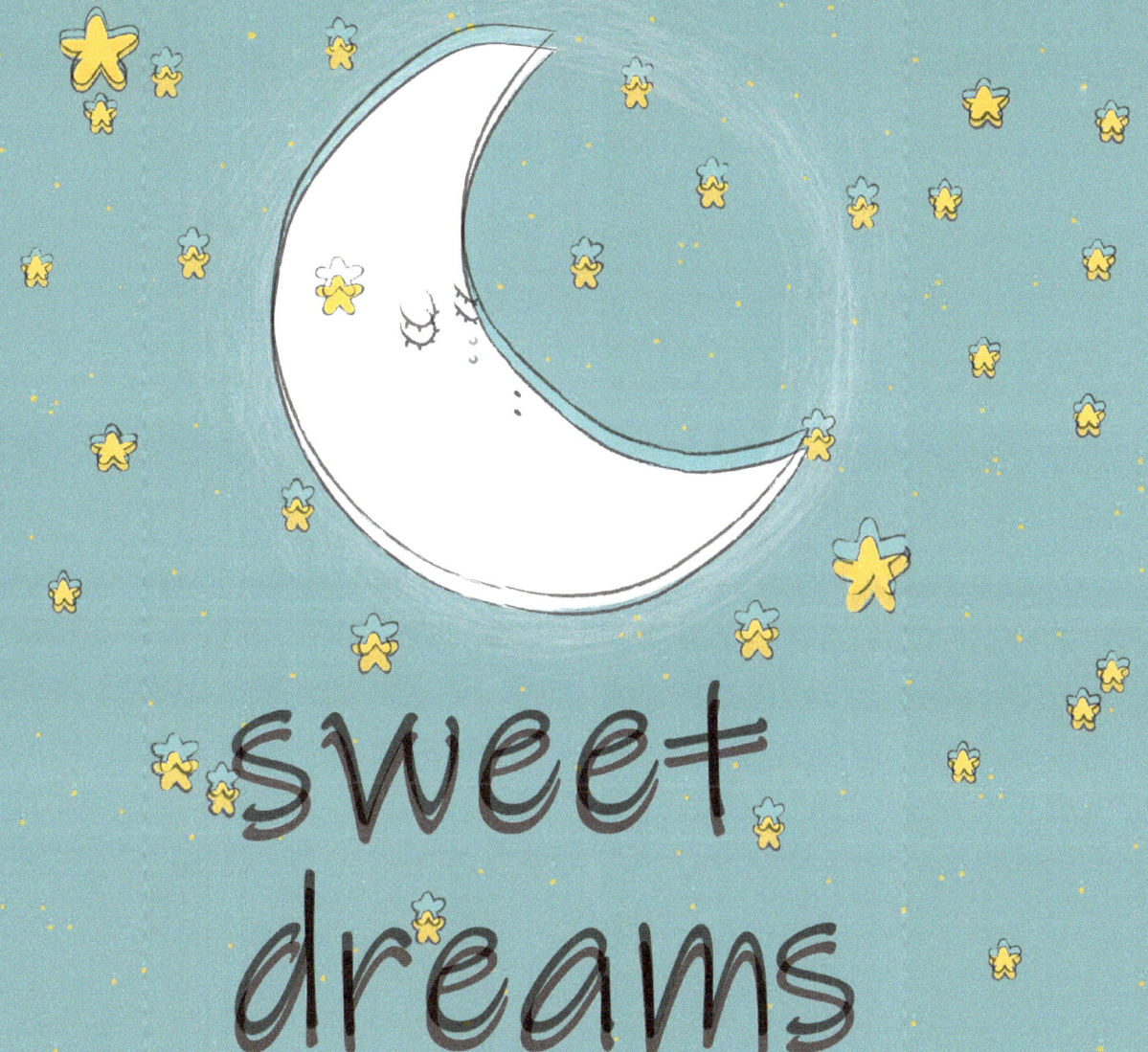

www.ingramcontent.com/pod-product-compliance
Lightning Source LLC
Chambersburg PA
CBHW051944210526
45473CB00006B/2371